the ULSter JOKE BOOK

Compiled by
Geoff Hill

Illustrated by
Maria

THE
BLACKSTAFF
PRESS

First published in 1987 by
The Blackstaff Press Limited
3 Galway Park, Dundonald, Belfast BT16 0AN, Northern Ireland
and
27 South Main Street, Wolfeboro, New Hampshire 03894 USA

Printed by The Guernsey Press Company Limited

British Library Cataloguing in Publication Data
    The Ulster joke book.
       1. English wit and humour.
       I. Hill, Geoff
       828'.91402'08   PN6175
ISBN 0-85640-392-X

This drunk jumps into a taxi in Belfast.

'Ladas Drive,' he says.

'No way,' says the driver. 'Sit in the back like everyone else.'

What do you call a junior Orangeman?

A pipsqueak.

Billy came down the stairs of his little terraced house in Belfast on Saturday morning wearing a pair of blue trousers, a red pullover, a white shirt with a blue tie, a Linfield scarf and rosette and a red, white and blue woolly hat, and carrying a football rattle.

'And where are you going?' asked his wife.

Seamus is sitting at home in his flat in Strabane when Aidan staggers through the door clutching four crates of Guinness and a sliced pan loaf.

'What are we having the party for, Aidan?' asks Seamus.

'We're not having a party, Seamus,' says Aidan.

'What have you bought all that bread for, then?'

Just before the election, the Unionist candidate was canvassing in west Belfast.

'I was born a Protestant, I live as a Protestant, and I am proud to say that I will die as a Protestant,' he told the gathered throng.

'Jaysus, man,' came a voice from the back of the crowd, 'have ye no ambition in ye at all?'

2

Two Belfast men go to Rome for their holidays. Naturally, after wandering around all day looking in vain for a fish and chip shop, they decide to go and get drunk.

So they find a pub and wander in and set themselves up at the bar – but they don't recognise any of the drinks on the shelves, and there's no sign of draught Bass about the place.

Undeterred, one of them summons the barman.

'Tell us, head-the-ball,' he says, 'what does the Pope drink when he goes out for the night?'

'Crème de menthe,' says the barman, recognising a right couple of eejits when he sees them.

'Right,' says the other Belfast man. 'If it's good enough for the Pope, it's good enough for us. We'll have two pints of crème de menthe.'

So they knock back the two pints of crème de menthe and order two more, and the next thing they know it's dawn the next day and they're waking up in the gutter with their mouths tasting like the outside toilets at a peppermint factory.

'Holy mother of God,' says one, 'if that's the stuff the Pope drinks, no wonder they carry him around in a chair all the time.'

What's the Ulster definition of passion?
Heavy rain in Ballymena.

What do they do about sex in Ballymena?
Have their tea.

This Belfast man, a fervent Catholic since the day he was born, went into his hairdressers up the Falls Road.

As he was having his short back, sides and front, the hairdresser got to chatting with him, as hairdressers will, and finally got around to asking him where he was going for the summer holidays, as hairdressers invariably do.

'I'm going to Rome in a week,' says yer man, 'and I'm tremendously excited about it, for it's me first trip.'

'Don't be,' says the hairdresser, snipping off a wee bit he hadn't noticed the first time around. 'The place is pigging, the food would make you sick and the women are one and all like the back end of a Citybus.'

'Ach well,' says yer man, 'I don't mind. As long as I get to see the Pope, I'll be happy enough.'

'See the Pope?' says the hairdresser, scrubbing in the Brylcreem. 'You haven't a mission. St Peter's Square is filled twenty-four hours a day with about ten million people, and when he comes out on the balcony all you can see is this tiny wee white dot the size of a pinhead.'

So yer man heads off to Rome anyway, and a month later he's back in the hairdressers for a trim.

'Well,' says the hairdresser, 'did you make it to Rome?'

'I did indeed,' says yer man.

'And was it as bad as I said?'

'Not a bit of it. It was as clean as a freshly painted doorstep, the food was so gorgeous it would have made ye weep, and the women were like something left behind by the angels.'

'That's amazing,' says the hairdresser. 'But did you see the Pope?'

'See him?' says yer man. 'Didn't he come down off the balcony and wander through the crowds, and wasn't I talking to him and even shook him by the hand?'

'You're not serious,' says the hairdresser. 'What did His Holiness say to you?'

'He said, "Where in the name of God did you get that haircut?"'

Billy went for a job and was asked if he'd filled in the questionnaire.

So he went outside and beat up the doorman.

Two Belfast women are walking past the Gramophone Shop in front of the City Hall when this music comes wafting out.

'That's Nat King Cole,' says one.

'Well, who is it then?' says the other.

St Peter is sitting at the gates of heaven one fine afternoon when this man arrives up in a well pressed blue suit and asks if there would be any chance of gaining admission.

'Well,' says St Peter, 'I didn't get where I am today by letting every Tom, Dick and Harry walk through these gates. What sort of virtuous qualities do you have which would make me want to let you in?'

'Well,' says yer man, 'I was very devout. I went to church every Sunday morning, well or ill, all my life, and lived as a good Christian every other day of the week.'

'Umm, that's a good start,' says St Peter, 'but it's hardly good enough. There are boyos in here who went to church once a day, and three times on Sundays, and had to walk fourteen miles there and back summer and winter with no soles on the shoes of their feet.'

'Well,' says yer man, 'what about fidelity? I never once looked at another woman in all the fifty years I was married. And before I was married I was as pure as the first day of spring.'

'Umm, that's highly commendable,' says St Peter, 'but you have to bear in mind that we're full to the brim in here with men of the cloth who spurned the sins of the flesh from the moment they were born until the day and hour they shuffled off their mortal coils.'

'I take your point,' says yer man. 'What about bravery then?'

'Umm, yes, bravery has a lot going for it,' says St Peter. 'What's your record on the courage front?'

'Well,' says yer man, 'once I walked almost the entire length of the Falls Road singing "The Sash" at the top of my voice and beating a Lambeg drum until I thought the skin would burst.'

'Oh?' says St Peter, 'and when was this, pray tell?'

'About five minutes ago,' says yer man.

What's a creche?
A car accident in Cherryvalley.

They don't have rates in Cherryvalley.
   They have mice.

This man walks into a bar up the Falls Road with a crocodile on a leash.

'Excuse me,' he says to the barman, 'do you serve Protestants?'

'Yes,' says the barman, 'we're fairly liberal.'

'Well,' says the customer, 'give me a pint of Guinness and two Protestants for the crocodile.'

An American was cruising through Co. Tyrone in his Cadillac when he stopped on the Carrickmore to Omagh road to watch the turf-cutting.

'Hey buddy,' he said to Liam, who was leaning on a fence, 'what's that little old machine over there?'

'That's our turf-digging machine,' said Liam.

'Really? Why, back in Texas we have spoons bigger than that,' said the American.

'Aye, but look at the size of your gub,' said Liam.

A Belfast man was walking through Roselawn Cemetery when he came upon a headstone inscribed: 'Here lies a politician and an honest man.'

'Boys-a-dear,' he said, 'I wonder how they got the two of them in the one grave?'

A Ballymena man went to the fancy-dress ball dressed as Napoleon so that he could keep his hand on his wallet.

A Belfast man was driving through the Antrim hills one dark night when he realised he had a puncture. He pulled up by the side of the road and knocked at the door of a nearby farmhouse to ask for help. When the farmer heard what had happened he gave a whistle, and this three-legged pig with a wooden leg hobbled out of one of the barns, went over to the car, and changed the wheel.

'That's amazing,' said the Belfast man.

'Oh, that's nothing,' said the farmer. 'Last month there was a fire in the barn and that pig leapt in and saved the lives of my wee son and daughter.'

'But tell me,' said the Belfast man, 'What happened to its leg?'

'Well,' said the farmer, 'You don't eat a pig like that all in one go.'

Two tigers were walking down Royal Avenue, when one turned to the other.

'It's very quiet for a Saturday, isn't it?' he said.

Jimmy's mother dragged him screaming into the doctor's surgery.

'Doctor, doctor,' she said, 'can a thirteen-year-old perform an appendicitis operation on himself?'

'Of course not,' said the doctor.

'You see?' said the mother. 'Now put it back, you wee brat.'

Ian Paisley needs a new suit. So he goes round all the tailors in Ballymena and the cheapest price he's quoted for a bespoke three-piece pinstripe is £150.

'This is ridiculous,' says the big man to himself. 'The last time I bought a suit it only cost me 3s.6d. I'll take myself up to Belfast and see if I can get a better deal there.'

So he goes round all the tailors on the Shankill Road and they all measure him up and calculate the amount of cloth they'll need to cover that ample frame, and the cheapest price any of them comes up with is £125.

'This is absolutely ridiculous,' says Paisley to himself. 'If my ain folk can't give me what I want at a decent price, I'll just have to go over to the other side and see what they come up with.'

So he sets off up the Falls and goes into the first tailors he sees. The tailor recognises him immediately, does a few quick calculations on the back of a Mass card and tells Paisley he can do him a suit for £35.

'That is absolutely astonishing, my Roman Catholic friend,' says Paisley. 'And can you tell me why the cheapest I can get a suit among the good Protestant people of this city is £125?'

'It's very easy, Mr Paisley,' says the tailor. 'You may be a big man up the Shankill, but you're not such a big man up here.'

On the day that the latest unemployment figures are announced in Strabane, this man is walking across the Lifford Bridge when he sees this other fella just about to leap off into the river. He rushes over and manages to catch him by the ankle as he jumps.

'Let me go, let me go,' cries the would-be suicide. 'I don't want to live.'

'I don't want to save you,' says the first man. 'I just want to know where you work.'

Did you hear about the North-West showband? They called themselves Limavadywaddy.

Derry jokes, for some reason, are particularly surreal. . .

For example, this drunk in Derry gets onto a bus.

'Does this bus go to Shantallow?' he inquires of the only other occupant.

'It was Wednesday yesterday,' is the reply.

'So am I. Do you fancy going for a pint?'

Or. . . How many Derry men does it take to screw in a lightbulb?

A fish.

While we're on the subject, how many Bangor solicitors does it take to screw in a lightbulb?

Bangor solicitors don't screw in lightbulbs, they screw in Jacuzzis.

How many Belfast folk singers does it take to screw in a lightbulb?

Ten. One to screw in the lightbulb and the other nine to sing about how good the old one was.

How many Gerry Adamses does it take to screw in a lightbulb?

None. Irish lightbulbs have a right to govern their own future.

How many Ulster politicians does it take to screw in a lightbulb?

Ten. One to screw in the lightbulb and the other nine to stop the ceiling falling into his mouth.

How many Cherryvalley teenagers does it take to screw in a lightbulb?

Two. One to mix a gin and tonic and the other to phone daddy.

Two farmers were leaning over a gate in the Sperrins when this American pulls up in the longest Cadillac you ever did see.

'Pardon me, gentlemen,' says the American, winding down the window, 'but could you tell me how far it is to O—magh.'

'Well now,' says one of the farmers, 'it would be the best part of fifteen miles from here. But in a car like that you should do it in ten.'

A Cullybackey dairy farmer heard on Downtown Radio that there was a bloodless coup in Uganda.

So he sent them a pint of blood from his own coo.

Sammy and Maisie from Dromore had been married for forty years, when Sammy came home one day all excited.

'Maisie, Maisie,' he said, 'I've just discovered we've been making love wrong all these years!'

'What d'ye mean, Sammy?' said Maisie.

'You're supposed to moan when we're doing it, Maisie.'

So that night they were lying in bed in a state of intimacy, and Sammy said: 'Right Maisie, start moanin' now.'

'Sammy, that ceiling could do wi' a new coat of paint,' said Maisie.

How do you know Jesus was from Strabane?

Because he had twelve mates who were all men, he lived at home until he was thirty-three, his mother thought he was God, and he thought his mother was a virgin.

A man is walking along the beach at Portrush when he happens upon two Protestants holding a rope which leads out to sea. On the other end of the rope is tied a Catholic, who's splashing and shouting and drowning and making a terrible fuss.

'Hold on a second, fellas,' says the passer-by, 'I'll give you a hand to save this poor drowning man.' So he grabs the rope from them and hauls the Catholic in.

As he's walking away, one Protestant turns to the other and says: 'Who the hell was that?'

'Haven't a clue,' said the other, picking up the gasping Catholic and throwing him back into the waves, 'but he doesn't seem to know much about shark-fishing.'

This nun is driving along in her Renault 5 when she has the misfortune to run out of petrol somewhere near Ahoghill.

So she jumps out of the car and walks down the road until she comes to a lane, and at the end of the lane there's a farm, and in the farmhouse there's a farmer, who, being a decent sort of bloke, siphons some petrol out of his Mercedes for her.

Unfortunately there isn't a petrol can about the place, and the only receptacle they can find, after a lengthy search of the premises, is a potty which was lying under a bed in one of the back rooms.

So the nun heads off with her potty full of

15

four-star, and walks back along the road until
she comes to the Renault.

Well, she's standing there carefully tipping
the contents into the petrol tank when who
should roll up but Ian Paisley in a motorcade on
his way to Stormont.

The armour-plated Granada slides to a halt
beside the Renault, and Paisley lowers the
electric window.

'Madam,' he says to the nun, 'I have no time
for your religion, but I can only admire your
faith.'

The phone rang in a Derry police station.
'Come quickly,' said the voice on the other end.
'Someone's broken into my house and stolen
the TV and the video and the stereo.'

A policeman was sent over to investigate.
'This is serious,' he said. 'The window's been
broken on both sides.'

This Derry man who's a fanatic about watches, but has never been able to afford one, wins a million in an accumulator at the bookies. So the first thing he does is get on a flight to London, go into the biggest jewellers he can find in Bond Street, and ask for the best watch in the shop.

'I think this is what sir is looking for,' says the smarmy assistant. 'It's solid gold and platinum, encrusted with diamonds; it took three years to make by the best craftsmen in Geneva, who destroyed the plans when they'd finished it; and inside it there is the finest in state-of-the-art timekeeping technology. You will never need to alter it from the moment you put it on, for it's guaranteed not to gain or lose a second for the next thousand years.

'I'll take it,' says the Derry man, writing out a cheque for £250,000.

So he gets the Shuttle back to Northern Ireland and that night he's sitting at home watching the TV when *News at Ten* comes on. He looks at the watch and it's showing a quarter past six.

Enraged, he jumps up and runs into the kitchen, where he finds his youngest son feeding the five greyhounds.

'You wee bugger,' he says, smacking him round the back of the head. 'Have you been messing around with that TV?'

Did you hear about the artificial insemination expert who visited a farm near Buckna? He knocked on the door and an old lady came out. He told her he was there to see to the cow, so she took him to the barn, opened the door and said: 'There you are, son. There's the coo and there's a nail on the back of the door to hang your trousers on.'

Two Derry men met on the Foyle Bridge.

'Have you seen Kevin recently?' asked Pat.

'I have and I haven't,' said Seamus.

'What do you mean?'

'Well, I was walking down the road when I saw this fella who I thought was Kevin, and he saw a fella who he thought was me. But when we got closer it was neither of us.'

The *Coleraine Chronicle* sent a reporter out to
interview the oldest man in Ulster.

'And what age are you exactly, Mr McGraw?'
asked the reporter.

'I'm wan hundred and three years old the day,
son,' said McGraw.

'And I'm sure you've seen a brave few changes in
your time?'

'I have indeed, son. And I've been against them
all.'

A Belfast couple were on honeymoon in Paris.
One night they were walking down the Boul
Mich when two fire engines and an ambulance
rushed past, their sirens blaring.

'Listen, darling,' said the husband. 'They're
playing our tune.'

Secretary of State Tom King is kneeling by his bed
in Hillsborough Castle one night praying to Maggie
Thatcher for divine guidance.

'Dear Maggie,' he prays, 'no matter how well I
do, the people in this place never give me any credit
for it. What can I do to become more popular?'

There is a distant hum and crackling of static,
and a voice booms like thunder from the ceiling:
'SUMMON THE PEOPLE TO THE RIVER.'

So next day Tom holds a press conference and
calls all the people of Northern Ireland to gather
along the banks of the Bann at noon the following
Monday.

On the Monday, the entire population of the
province – except for a couple of Bangor solicitors,

who are on holiday in the Bahamas – turn up on the banks of the Bann to see what's going to happen. After a few minutes a helicopter emerges from the cloud and lands and Tom gets out looking a little nervous behind the horn-rimmed spectacles.

'What now, Maggie?' he asks.

'NOW WALK OVER THE WATER,' booms the voice from the clouds.

Hesitantly, Tom approaches the water's edge and steps onto the river. And lo and behold, he is able to walk all the way across. . .

Exultant, he has almost reached the other bank when he hears a low grumbling from the crowd.

'Typical,' it says. 'The man can't even swim.'

Why is sex before marriage frowned upon in Ulster?

Because it crumples the wedding dress and makes you late for the service.

The phone rang in a Ballymena pub, and the owner picked it up.

'This is the Provos,' said a voice at the other end. 'The place is bombed and you've got five minutes to get out.'

The owner put down the phone and went to the bar.

'Last orders, everyone,' he said.

In one of his early sermons in the vicinity of Sixmilecross, Ian Paisley took as his text a quotation from St Paul's Epistle to the Ephesians.

After the service was over, he was standing outside shaking hands with all and sundry when he was approached by a very old, venerable and deaf Orangeman.

'That was a powerful good service, young Paisley,' quavers the old man, 'powerful good. And I must say I liked thon bit about St Paul taking a pistol to the Fenians.'

The newly wed Free Presbyterian entered the bridal suite and found his new bride lounging in a negligee on top of the duvet.

'I had hoped that I would find you on your knees by the side of the bed, dear,' he said disapprovingly.

'Well, I will if you want me to, but I always get the hiccups doing it that way,' said the bride.

A Derry man walks into a pub with a door under his arm.

'What's with the door, Pat?' asks the barman.

'Oh, I lost my key last night.'

'Well what happens if you lose the door?'

'That's no problem. I left the window open.'

A ventriloquist on a UK tour was going down great guns in the Grand Opera House in Belfast with a string of jokes about the Welsh, the Scots, the English and the Americans.

'Now,' he said, 'to finish off, I'm sure you won't mind if I tell a joke about the people here.'

At this point a rather large gentleman got up in the front circle and said: 'We'll have none of that. We are not as stupid here as people think we are.'

'Don't worry, sir,' said the ventriloquist, 'I can assure you that the joke will not be in the least offensive.'

'I'm not talking to you,' said the heckler, 'I'm talking to that wee fella on your knee.'

This man walked into a pub in Larne with a wee scabby dog under his arm, just in time to hear the Saturday afternoon soccer results on the radio.

'Linfield three, Larne nil.' said the announcer, at which point the dog shouted: 'Oh no!' and started bawling his head off.

More than astonished, the barman leaned over the counter and said: 'Here, mate, your dog just shouted "Oh no!"'

'I know,' said the dog's owner. 'He always does that when Larne lose.'

'What does he do when they win?' asked the barman.

'I don't know,' said the owner. 'I've only had him for a year and a half.'

Two IRA men were on their way to blow up a pub.

'What happens if the bomb goes off before we get there?' said O'Rourke.

'It's all right,' said McSwiggan. 'I have a spare in the boot.'

A priest was walking down a street in Cookstown when he came across a little girl struggling to reach a door knocker.

'Here, my dear, let me help,' he said, striding manfully up and giving the door a good batter with his walking stick.

'That's it,' said the little girl. 'Now run like hell.'

What do most of the burns patients in Belfast hospitals have in common?

They're all UVF explosives experts.

This is a true story which happened to a friend of mine. He went into an off-licence up the Shankill one evening and asked for two bottles of wine and a couple of cans of beer.

The girl rang them up in the till.

'£10.66,' she said.

'Oh,' I said, 'the Battle of Hastings!'

She thought for a minute. 'I don't think we have any bottles of Hastings, mister.'

An American tourist was driving through Ahoghill when his Cadillac ground to a halt for no obvious reason.

He got out and walked into the nearest shop.

'Pardon me, friend, but are there any mechanics living around here?' he said.

'No, we're all McDonalds,' said the assistant.

Two Limavady men were up for their first trip in an aeroplane.

'Kieran,' said one to the other, 'if this machine turns upside down, would we fall out?'

'Don't be silly, Liam,' said Kieran, 'we'll always be friends.'

A Ballymena man died and arrived at the pearly gates. Naturally enough, before St Peter would let him in, he had to have some evidence of good deeds carried out during his time on earth.

'Well,' said the Ballymena man, 'once on Christmas Eve I gave 2p to an old woman in the snow. Mind you, I'd knocked her down in my Mercedes, but I could have just driven on.'

'I see,' said St Peter. 'Anything else?'

'Once I gave a penny to a little blind boy whose parents were killed in an accident at my Bible publishing plant.'

'I see,' said St Peter. 'I'll just have to check this with Gabriel.' So he picked up the phone and got through to Gabriel and gave him the details.

'Give him back his 3p and tell him to go to hell,' said Gabriel.

The phone rings in a flat in Strabane.

'Hello, hello, is that Liam?'

'No, it's Paddy.'

'Oh, sorry, I must have a wrong number.'

'That's all right, I wasn't in anyway.'

A young married couple wanted to buy a house in Bangor. So they went to see the snootiest estate agent in town.

'Right,' said the estate agent. 'Just tell me what price you were thinking of, then we'll all have a good laugh and take it from there.'

Two Provos met at the crossroads in the middle of the night.

'What time is it, Liam?' said Pat.

'I don't know,' said Liam. 'My time-bomb's fast.'

This ma drags her wee lad into a clothes shop in Belfast and asks for a t-shirt with a 'Q' on it. The shop assistant looks and looks but eventually admits defeat.

'I'm sorry, Madam, we don't seem to have one.'

'There, what did I tell ye, Qhughie?'

It was Sunday in Ballyclare and the service was being taken by a young clergyman just up from Belfast. Rising to his full height in the pulpit, he said: 'Friends, I am preaching today on the sin of adultery. If there are any among you who have committed this sin, let his tongue cleave to the woof of his mowf.'

Ulster International Airlines were having a little trouble on their first flight to New York.

Captain O'Reilly turned to his co-pilot as they approached Kennedy Airport and said: 'It looks from here as if they've only given us a very short runway. We're going to need a really steep descent, then brakes slammed on and engines full in reverse.'

'Roger,' said the co-pilot.

'The name's Patrick,' said Captain O'Reilly, preparing to land.

The jumbo came screaming down almost vertically, pulled out at the last minute, hit the tarmac with brakes locked and engines screaming like banshees, and shuddered to a halt half an inch from the edge of the runway.

Captain O'Reilly and his crew got out to inspect the landing.

'That was a close shave,' said O'Reilly. 'I've never seen such a short runway in all my born days.'

'Neither have I,' said the co-pilot. 'But look at the width of it.'

Rodney was a Bangor solicitor, and one night his wife, Samantha, was in bed with Rodney's best friend, James, when the phone rang. Samantha reached over, picked up the receiver and had a brief conversation.

'Who was that?' asked James.

'It was Rodney. He phoned to say he'd be late because he was going out to the golf club for a drink with you and the lads.'

Four Strabane men were sent out near Newtownstewart one day to dig a hole in the road for the Department of the Environment. But when they arrived they discovered that they only had two shovels, so one of them went up to complain to the foreman.

'Listen,' said the foreman. 'If you're short of shovels, just lean against each other.'

A top Provisional IRA man was shot by the Army and arrived at the pearly gates.

'And who might you be?' asked St Peter.

'O'Reilly of the west Belfast active service unit.'

'Well, you're wasting your time trying to get in here.'

'I don't want to get in. You've got ten minutes to get out.'

A Protestant walked into a bar up the Shankill with a pig under his arm.

'Where did you get that?' said the barman.

'I won him in a raffle,' said the pig.

Two Queen's students were trying to decide what to do that evening.

'I know,' said one. 'We'll toss a coin. Heads we'll go to the downstairs bar in the Students' Union and spend our grants, tails we'll go to the upstairs bar and spend our grants.'

'What happens if it lands on the edge?' asks the other.

'Then we'll just have to stay in and study.'

Who invented limbo dancing?

A Ballymena man trying to get into a pay toilet.

This man is walking home from the pub, through the Markets in Belfast, when a masked man steps out of an alleyway and points a gun at his head.

'Are you a Taig or a Prod?' asks the gunman.

Terrified of giving the wrong answer, the man thinks for a minute, and then says: 'I'm Jewish, actually.'

'Really?' says the gunman. 'In that case, I must be the luckiest Arab in the city tonight.'

Three clergymen, one from Belfast, one from Derry and one from Ballymena, were discussing how to make a little profit out of the Sunday collection.

'Well,' said the Belfast clergyman, 'after I've taken all the collection I just dip my hand in and take a handful, and that does me.'

'I think that's erring a little on the righteous side,' said the Derry clergyman. 'I think it's fairer to divide it in half.'

'Not at all,' said the Ballymena clergyman. 'The most Christian way is to throw all the money up in the air. What stays up is God's, and what comes back down is mine.'

Downtown Radio newsflash. . . 'A store in Stranraer was broken into last night. The only items taken were an umbrella and forty packets of best birdseed. Larne police are on the lookout for a budgie on a walking tour of Northern Ireland.'

A Cullybackey woman got onto the Belfast express, and all the seats were taken.

Eventually a farmer's son who'd had politeness beaten into him got up and offered her his place.

'Thanks very much, son,' she said. 'But I daren't sit down, I'm in that much of a hurry.'

A Ballymena man arrives at a toll bridge with his son in the passenger seat of the Mercedes.

'That's £1 for the car and 50p for the passenger,' says the attendant.

'Make it 50p for the car and I'll throw in the boy for free,' says the Ballymena man.

Two Ballymena men won the pools and were celebrating their winnings in the pub.

'There's only one thing,' said Bob. 'What are we going to do with all the begging letters?'

'Don't worry,' said Billy, 'I'll post them on the way home.'

An SAS man was sent to south Armagh to try and rout the IRA active service unit in a small village near Crossmaglen. He was to make contact with a mole called O'Reilly, and the password was: 'Isn't it dreadful weather for June?'

So, he was dropped by helicopter two miles from the village in the early morning, and he walked there across the heathery hills, to arrive just as the shops were opening. He thought he would start hunting for his contact by looking for any shops called O'Reilly's. But as he walked down the single street, all he could see was O'Reilly's Butcher, O'Reilly's Chemist, O'Reilly's Hardware Store, O'Reilly's Jacuzzi Supplies. . .

Stumped, he walked into O'Reilly's pub, which was open despite the early hour. O'Reilly the publican was leaning on the well-polished bar, and the SAS man ordered a pint of stout from him. The two of them chatted away, and the publican was so friendly that after a while the SAS man wondered if, after all, this could be the O'Reilly he was looking for.

'Actually, the reason I'm here,' he said tentatively, is to. . . ah. . . look for an old friend called O'Reilly.'

'Ah, well,' said the publican, 'as you can see, they're all O'Reillys around here. Which one was it you were looking for?'

What the hell, thought the SAS man. In at the deep end, and all that. . . So he leaned across the bar and whispered: 'Isn't it dreadful weather for June?'

'Ah yes,' said the publican, 'It was O'Reilly the mole you were looking for.'

What's the fastest game in the world?
Pass the parcel in a Belfast pub.

A Derry man staggered into the casualty area at Altnagelvin Hospital.

'Help,' he said. 'I've accidentally swallowed 200 aspirin.'

'Good grief,' said the nurse. 'When was this?'

'Friday night.'

'Don't be silly. Today's Monday so if you took them on Friday night you'd be dead by now.'

'Maybe it was Thursday, then.'

FLAHERTY

In *University Challenge,* the score with a minute to go was Oxford 480, Queen's nil.

Feeling sorry for the underdogs, Bamber Gascoigne said: 'Right, Queen's, here's your starter for ten. Complete the following sequence – One, two, three. . .'

Buzzzzzz.

'Queen's Flaherty,' said Bamber.

'O'Leary,' said Flaherty.

It was Christmas Day in Bangor and the elderly clergyman was standing by the handsome fire waiting for his four sons to come down to breakfast.

The first son came into the room, adjusting his dog collar.

'Good morning, father,' he said.

'Good morning, my son,' said the clergyman. 'And did you spend a comfortable night?'

'Wonderful, father. I dreamt of heaven, and it was just like home.'

He joined his father by the fire, and both proceeded to toast their nether regions and gaze out through the leaded windows at the flurries of snow. After a few minutes the second son came down, also in his dog collar, and the same conversation took place. Eventually the third son, also a clergyman, walked through the door, and said much the same thing as the first two.

So all four of them were standing by the fire warming themselves when the door opened and the fourth son walked in wearing his pinstripe suit and spotted tie. A solicitor, he was not only the black sheep of the family, but earned more than the rest of them put together.

'Morning, father,' he said.

'Good morning,' said his father. 'Sleep well?'

'Oh, all right,' said the fourth son. 'I spent most of the night having this dream about hell.'

'Really? What was it like?'

'Just like home. You couldn't get near the fire for the bloody clergy.'

A Belfast man was ashamed of his accent, and decided to go to elocution lessons in London.

Three years later he was speaking perfect BBC English, and he decided to return home and celebrate with a drink.

He caught the Shuttle to Belfast, got a taxi into the city and walked into the first establishment he came to.

'I say, old chap,' he said to the proprietor, 'perhaps you could furnish me with a large gin and tonic and one of your finest Havana cigars.'

'You're from around these parts, aren't you?' said the proprietor.

'Good grief,' said the stunned Belfast man. 'How did you know that?'

'Well, you see,' said the proprietor, 'this is a butcher's.'

The bank in west Belfast had just opened when a masked and armed man burst through the door.

'Empty the tills or else,' he said.

'Or else what?' asked the cashier.

'Ah. . . I'm not sure. Can I call back tomorrow?'

A Lisburn woman bought her husband *The Joy of Sex* for Christmas.

He coloured it in.

Ulster dyslexics say 'On'.

Two shipyard workers were walking home
from Harland's one day and it started to rain.
One of them immediately took off his cap and
stuffed it in his pocket.

'What are you doing that for?' his mate
asked.

'Well I can't go to bed in a wet cap.'

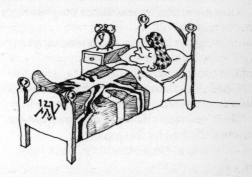

The matron walked into a ward at the Royal
Victoria Hospital and saw a man wrapped in
bandages from head to toe.

'What on earth happened to you, young man?'
she said.

'Well, matron,' he mumbled through the
bandages. 'I'm a member of the English skiing
team, and we were taking part in the British
championships at the Craigavon ski slope this
morning.'

'And did you fall?' said the matron.

'No. We met the Northern Ireland team
coming up.'

This nun at the Sacred Heart of St Brigid's Primary School is asking all the kids in her class what they are going to be when they grow up.

The first one she comes to is little Patrick.

'I'm going to be a priest, sister,' says little Patrick – the crawler.

'God bless you, little Patrick,' says the nun, passing on to the desk where little Concepta sits.

'I'm going to be a nun and a teacher like you,' says little Concepta – the brat.

'God bless you, little Concepta,' says the nun, passing on to the seat on which is placed the behind of little Derval, who comes from a family of fourteen living in a caravan which was abandoned by the gypsies.

'I'm going to be a prostitute,' says little Derval.

'Whaaaat?' squeals the nun, clutching her rosary beads for support and turning forty shades of puce.

'I said I'm going to be a prostitute,' says little Derval.

'Thanks be to God.' says the nun, 'I thought you said a Protestant.'

At Cherryvalley High, meanwhile, Miss Fotheringill is asking the good little boys and girls of first year what their fathers do, so that the headmistress can mark out the future prefects.

'My daddy is a judge, Miss Fotheringill,' says

little Samantha, brushing back the royal blue bow which holds her mane of freshly-washed blonde locks.

'Very good, Samantha dear,' says Miss Fotheringill, placing a discreet tick beside little Samantha's name in her big black book before moving on to the desk of little Roland.

'My daddy's a consultant surgeon, Miss Fotheringill,' says little Roland, his big blue eyes filled with the innocence of freshly clipped church lawns.

'That's very nice, Roland dear,' says Miss Fotheringill, marking little Roland down as a future head boy and moving on to the desk of little Jimmy, whose father is a bookmaker. Miss Fotheringill does not know this, but the tattoo of a swallow flitting across little Jimmy's neck has already drawn her to the conclusion that little Jimmy is definitely not future officer material.

'My da's dead,' lies little Jimmy.

'Oh dear,' says Miss Fotheringill, overcome with remorse for her unkind thoughts about the poor lad. 'And what did he do before he died, little James?'

'He grabbed his throat and went "Aaaarrrrggghhhh", Miss.'

This worm was swallowed by a cow in a field near Ahoghill. As it lay in the cow's stomach wondering how to escape, it fell asleep. When it woke up, the cow wasn't there.

Chief Inspector McSwiggan arrived at Ballymena RUC station for his first day in charge, and gathered the entire contingent together for a lecture on riot control and crowd dispersal.

'I'm sure you all realise that we could be faced with a long hot summer of riots over this new Public Order Order,' he said. 'So I've asked headquarters to send us twenty armoured Land-rovers, 500 plastic bullet guns and 100,000 baton rounds for crowd-dispersal purposes.'

'Waste of time,' came a muttered voice from the back of the room.

'Stand up that man!' roared the chief inspector. 'What is your name, constable?'

· 'Bloggs, sir,' said Constable Bloggs, shuffling to his feet.

'So, Bloggs,' said the chief inspector, 'you think it's a waste of time sending for all this extra and very necessary equipment which could very well save the lives of you and your fellow officers in an emergency?'

'I do, sir.'

'Well, Bloggs. Let us imagine for a moment that you are standing alone in the middle of Ballymena, confronted by an angry crowd of 10,000, hurling petrol bombs, bricks and the spare wheels of Volvos. How exactly would you got about dispersing this mob?'

'I would take off my hat, sir, and threaten to pass it round.'

Three Ballymena men were left £1,000 each by an old friend. The only condition was that they had to throw a tenner each into the grave as the coffin was being lowered.

The first man threw in a tenner that he'd borrowed from the wife of the dead man. The second man threw in a tenner that he'd borrowed from the third man. The third man fished out the two tenners, wrote out a cheque for £30, and threw that in.

Three days later he got a statement from his bank telling him that the cheque had been cashed.

The undertaker was a Ballymena man as well.

An American tourist was doing the troublespots in west Belfast. He arrived at Divis Flats and was walking past a shop when he noticed that there was nothing in the window but electric guitars and revolvers. Intrigued, he went inside.

'Tell me, buddy,' he said to the owner, 'do you ever sell any of those?'

'Oh yes,' said the owner. 'Every time we sell an electric guitar, one of the neighbours comes in and buys a gun.'

Two Ulster farmhands were standing in a field when a flock of birds flew over.

'Oh look,' said one. 'Gulls.'

'Don't be daft,' said the other. 'How can you tell what sex they are from this distance?'

A good citizen of Castlereagh was on his way home from church when he came across a man lying in the middle of the road, covered in blood.

'Good heavens, man, what happened to you?' he asked.

'The engine of my plane blew up and I had to bale out,' said the man. 'But my parachute didn't open.'

'Ah yes,' said the Castlereagh man. 'You'll find that nothing opens around here on Sunday.'

Did you hear about the Ballymena psychiatrist? He only treats schizophrenics. It means he can send them two bills every month.

One day another Ballymena man came in. The psychiatrist treated him for an hour, and at the end of it told him that he was a schizophrenic.

'That'll be £20,' he said.

'Here's £10,' said the patient. 'The other fella can look after himself.'

A Ballymena man, on the holiday of a lifetime in the Holy Land, arrived at the Sea of Galilee and inquired of the waiting boatman how much it would be to take a little trip.

'£10,' said the boatman.

'£10?' said the Ballymena man. 'At home I could buy a boat for that.'

'But these are the waters upon which our dear Lord walked,' protested the boatman.

'I'm not surprised, at those prices,' said the Ballymena man.

The Provos were planning the takeover of Derry.

'Right, Liam,' said the CO of the active service unit. 'I want you to take Seamus and Francie and immobilise the train station so that the Brits can't use it.'

An hour later Liam came back with a large sack.

'That was quick,' said the CO. 'Did you do a good job?'

'Sure,' said Liam. 'I got all the tickets.'

A policeman from Cullybackey is transferred to Belfast, and on his first night out on the beat he comes across a drunk lying down the street from the City Hall.

Being a fair cop, he gets out the notebook and pencil to write a report before taking the drunk in.

So he's standing there writing away laboriously when a passer-by walks past, as passers-by tend to.

'Excuse me, sir,' says the constable, 'but could you tell me what street we're in?'

'Why yes,' says the passer-by, 'This is Chichester Street.'

'Ay right,' says the constable, scratching his head. 'You wouldn't give us a hand to move him into May Street, would you?'

Two Cookstown men saved up all year and went to Blackpool for a week for their holidays. They had a wild time gorging themselves on pink rock and milk stout and running around in Kiss-Me-Quick hats playing all the video machines. . .

Such a wild time, in fact, that by the Friday they only had a quid between them and a whole day to spend before the coach left for Belfast that night.

'I tell you what,' says one to the other, 'take the quid and go down to the shops and buy a pack of cards or something to keep us amused. It'll give us something to do.'

So his mate goes down to the shops and comes back five minutes later with a packet of Tampax.

'What the hell did you get these for?' asks the first fella.

'Well,' says his mate, 'look at the side of the packet. It says we can go swimming, or horse-riding, or play tennis. . .'

An IRA active service unit was waiting in the undergrowth in the wilds of south Armagh for a British Army patrol to pass by.

'What time is it?' says one.

'Half past four,' says the other.

'That's funny. The patrol was due here at four o'clock,' says the first. 'I hope nothing's happened to them.'

What's black and white and hides in a cave?
A nun with an overdraft.

The Royal Irish Rangers were on jungle patrol in Belize when they came to a crocodile-infested river which they had to cross to get back to camp. After three men had been killed trying to swim across with a rope, Sergeant O'Reilly turned to the two Belfast men in the platoon.

'I'm afraid it's going to have to be one of you two,' he said.

'That's all right, sir,' said Billy. 'I'm sure Sammy will go.'

'I don't mind, sir,' said Sammy. 'I'm not afraid.'

So Sammy got the rope between his teeth, stripped off and dived in.

'Well,' said the sergeant, 'that's the last you'll see of him.'

'Not at all, sir,' said Billy. 'Here's a tenner says he'll make it.'

The money changed hands, and the next thing they saw was Sammy clambering up the far bank with the rope in his teeth.

'My God,' said Sergeant O'Reilly. 'How did you know he would make it?'

'It was easy, Sergeant. He's a Larne supporter, you see.'

'So?'

'Well, he's got "Larne for the Cup" tattooed on one buttock and "Larne are the next League Champions" tattooed on the other, and not even a crocodile would swallow that.'

Two Cullybackey farmers were slowly negotiating their tractor and haycart out of a field when a Bangor solicitor in his white Maserati came roaring over the hill doing about 120 mph and saw the tractor pulling into the road in front of him.

He slammed on the brakes, but he was going too fast and the car skidded into the field and burst into flames.

One of the farmers turned to the other. 'God save us,' he said, 'but we got out of that field just in time.'

They've banned the teabreaks on Co. Tyrone building sites.

It takes too long to retrain the workers.

A Fermanagh man was standing on the bridge near Kesh watching an American fishing, and he noticed that before each cast the American dipped the bait into a bottle which he kept by his side.

The local was astonished when five minutes later the American had half a dozen fine trout flapping on the shore beside him.

Intrigued, he walked down to the river's edge and asked the visitor what was the secret of his success.

'It's no secret, friend,' said the American. 'This here is a good old bottle of the finest Kentucky bourbon. The fish just go crazy for it.'

So the local rushed back to his little cottage and dug out his fishing rod from the parlour. Not having any Kentucky bourbon, however, he hoked out a bottle of poteen and decided that would do just as well.

Later that day the American was on his way back to his hotel when he met the local coming the other way with a salmon the size of a baby elephant slung over his shoulder.

'Well, friend, I see the old bourbon trick worked for you too,' said the American.

'You should try poteen instead,' said the local. 'When I got this boyo out of the water it took me five minutes to get the worm to let go of his throat.'

Queen's University's archaeology department has just unearthed a 1644 penny in a dig outside Ballymena.

A few feet away they found three skeletons on their hands and knees.

Two Derry men were on their way to a fancy-dress party, dressed as herrings, when they decided to step into a pub on the way for a pint.

They sat at the bar for a while, and then one of them got up and walked out the front door without finishing his pint.

When he hadn't come back after ten minutes, the barman came over and said: 'Hi, where's your mate vanished to?'

'How should I know?' replied the other Derry man. 'Am I my brother's kipper?'

49

A Belfast man went into a chemist's and asked for a comb.

'Do you wanna steel one, mister?' asked the assistant.

'Naw, it's all right, I'll pay for it.'

Fed up with hunting for work in Strabane, Liam went to Belfast to look for a job.

At the end of the second week, he was running out of money and hadn't eaten for three days. Desperate with the thought of going back to Strabane, he decided to head up to Belfast Zoo and commit suicide by jumping into the polar bear enclosure.

But just as he was saying the Last Rites to himself, one of the zookeepers rushed up to him and said: "Listen, do you want a job?'

'Thank God,' said Liam. 'My prayers have been answered.'

'Well,' said the zookeeper, 'it's like this. Clive, our prize gorilla, has just snuffed it, and with the waiting list for gorillas these days we won't get another one until Christmas the year after next.'

'So where do I fit in?' asked Liam.

'We have an old gorilla skin lying in the store. If you put it on, no one will know the difference.'

'And what's the pay like?'

'£100 a week.'

'I'll take it,' said Liam.

Well, so glad was he to get the job that he launched into it with terrific gusto, and after a few days his acrobatics on the branches had made the gorilla enclosure the most popular part of the zoo.

Inspired by the applause, Liam grabbed the top bar of the cage, did a somersault – and went sailing right over the top into the middle of the lion pen.

'Dear God,' said Liam 'I'm going to be eaten alive.'

'If you'd just shut up,' said one of the lions, 'we might all keep our jobs.'

A Larne supporter came home on a lovely summer's day dripping wet.

'What happened?' said his wife.

'The manager of the other team flooded the pitch so he could bring on his sub.'

'I've never been able to understand,' said the Belfast man reading page two of the *News Letter*, 'how people always die in alphabetical order.'

Sammy from Belfast goes to Las Vegas for his holidays, and goes to see Frank Sinatra at the Golden Thingummy. Halfway through the night he's standing in the toilet when who should come in but the man himself.

'Excuse me, Mr Sinatra,' says Sammy, 'but I wonder if you wouldn't mind doing me a favour.'

'Sure,' says Frank. 'What is it?'

'Well,' says Sammy, 'I've met this beautiful blonde and I'm trying to chat her up. It would impress her a lot if you come down through the dinner tables at the end of your show and say "Hi Sammy" as you're passing our table.'

'No problem,' says Frank, zipping himself up.

So Sammy goes back to his table and Frank goes back up on stage, and after he's finished three encores of 'My Way' he strolls down through the tables, welcoming the gratuitous accolades of the gathered throng. And as he's passing Sammy's table he gives a big cheery smile and says: 'Hi there Sammy, my old buddy.'

'Piss off, Frank,' says Sammy. 'Can't you see I'm with someone?'

Billy and George were driving into Larne to watch a match when a tyre burst and they swerved into a tree. George was all right, but Billy, who hadn't been wearing his seatbelt, was flung out on the road and fractured his skull.

Distraught, George ran like the blazes to the nearest phone box and phoned for an ambulance.

'Is there anything I can do before you get here?' he asked the hospital.

'The best thing you can do is support Billy's head,' said the doctor.

Five minutes later the ambulance screeched to a halt at the scene of the accident and found Billy lying moaning in the road and George jumping up and down beside him shouting and clapping: 'Billy's head – rarara – Billy's head – rarara.'

What are the best ten years of a Strabane man's life?

Primary One.

The psychiatrist walked into the ward at Purdysburn and found a new admission.

'Oh, and what are you in for?' he said.

'I like sausages,' said the man.

'But there's nothing wrong with that,' said the psychiatrist. 'I like sausages, too.'

'Really? Do you want to come home and see my collection?'

Liam and Concepta lived in a wee cottage out in the wilds of the Sperrins. One night Concepta, who was in an extremely advanced state of pregnancy, was taken sick while she was out in the barn putting the cattle in for the night.

Liam told her to stay where she was, and ran like hell to the phone box a mile down the road to phone for Dr O'Reilly.

Half-an-hour later the doctor pulled up outside the barn in his Morris Traveller, and came running in.

'Just in time,' he said. 'Get me lashings of hot water – and a candle so I can see what I'm going.'

So Liam ran and boiled the water and came running back out to the barn with a bucketful and the candle. He had no sooner arrived to the door than there was a smack and a wail.

'Congratulations, Liam,' said Dr O'Reilly. 'You're the father of a grand wee boy.'

'Thanks be to God,' said Liam. 'I'll go into the house and get the bottle of poteen and we'll have a wee sup.'

'Wait a minute,' said the doctor. 'Just hold that candle a bit closer.'

Liam did what he was told, and a minute later there was another smack and a wail.

'Congratulations, Liam,' said the doctor. 'It's twins!'

'Thanks be to God,' said Liam. 'Forget the sup. I'll bring out the whole bottle.'

'Wait a minute,' said the doctor. 'Just hold that candle a bit closer.'

A minute later there was a smack and a wail.

'Well, I'll be a monkey's uncle,' said the doctor. 'It's triplets!'

'Thanks be to God,' said Liam. 'Forget the bottle. We'll get all the neighbours round and we'll have a hooley!'

'Wait a minute,' said the doctor. 'Just hold that candle a bit closer.'

'I don't want to be awkward, doctor,' said Liam, 'but do you think it's this damned light's attracting them?'

A Ballymena man counted his change six times at the shop counter.

· 'What's the matter?' asked the assistant. 'Didn't I give you enough?'

'Yes, but only just.'

Two Strabane men had been shipwrecked on an iceberg for six months in 1912 when one turned to the other.

'We're saved,' he said. 'Here comes the *Titanic!*'

A Ballymena man went out of the house on Christmas Eve and fired a single shot, then came back in and told his children that Santa Claus had committed suicide.

Why do traffic wardens have a yellow stripe around their hats?

To stop people parking on their heads.

Three Ballymena men went to one of Ian Paisley's services for the first time. Halfway through the service, Paisley announced that the collection would be taken.

'Nothing less than a fiver, friends,' be boomed from the pulpit.

One of the Ballymena men fainted on the spot, and the other two carried him out.

Why did the Ballymena man buy a black and white dog?

Because the licence was cheaper.

How do you get a Ballymena man onto the roof?

Tell him the drinks are on the house.

A man got on a bus in Derry, and was just sitting there quietly when his neighbour took a piece of string out of his pocket, walked up to the front of his bus and started dangling it in front of the driver. The driver immediately burst into tears, and the man put the piece of string back into his pocket and returned to his seat.

'That driver,' he said, 'he's got no sense of humour at all.'

'What do you mean?' said the Derry man.

'They're hanging his brother tomorrow.'

'Bridget, Kevin's just been run over by a steamroller.'

'I'm in the bath. Just slide him under the door.'

Downtown Radio newsflash. . . 'Ian Paisley was rushed to hospital last night in Ballymena. He was out walking when he was run over by a speedboat.'

Liam was on his way to music class when he was lifted by the police and whisked off to Castlereagh.

After ten minutes a detective came into the cell.

'All right, Liam,' he said. 'What are the pieces of paper with the code on them we found in your bag?'

'They're by Sibelius,' said Liam.

After four days without food or water, he had another visit from the detective.

'All right, Liam,' he said. 'You might as well come clean. Sibelius has already confessed.'

Liam is walking down the Falls Road in Belfast when he meets Kevin.

'Ao, eam,' says Kevin, with difficulty.

'What have you got in your mouth?' asks Liam.

'A grenade,' says Kevin, taking it out to show him. 'One of the Brits punched me in the gub yesterday, and if he tries it again today he'll get his hand blown off.'

Three Ballymena men got on a train together, and sat down in the same carriage.

As the train rattled towards Belfast, one of them got out a pipe and started filling it. When he'd finished he turned to one of the others and said: 'You wouldn't have a match on you, at all?'

'I haven't a single match on me,' said the second man, sitting very still so that the matchbox in his pocket wouldn't make a sound.

The man with the pipe turned to the third occupant of the carriage. 'What about you?' he said.

'You needn't be looking at me,' said the man, cursing the fact that he wouldn't be able to enjoy a cigarette on the whole journey. 'I don't smoke.'

The man with the pipe started to cry. 'Dammit,' he said, 'I suppose I'll have to use one of my own.'

How do you tell a Ballymena restaurant?

There are forks in the sugar bowl.

An Englishman was walking through the Markets in Belfast late at night when the inevitable masked and armed man jumped out of an alleyway.

'Give us your money!' demanded the gunman.'

'Certainly not,' said the Englishman, knocking the gun out of his hand and jumping on him.

The two of them fought for three hours, until finally the gunman got his hands on the Englishman's wallet and opened it. Three moths from an extinct species flew out, and in the bottom of it he found 3p.

'Good God, man,' said the gunman. 'Do you mean to tell me you fought me for three hours to save yourself 3p?'

'Not at all,' said the Englishman. 'I thought you were after the £500 in my shoe.'

Why are 50p pieces the shape they are?

So you can use a spanner to get them off a Ballymena man.

The minister was driving his car through Cookstown when he came out of a side road without looking and ran slap bang into the priest's Mercedes.

'Heavens above, Father,' he said, 'I'm dreadfully sorry. Are you all right?'

'Oh, nothing broken,' said the priest. 'I'm just a bit shaken, that's all.'

'I have the very thing,' said the minister, producing a silver hip flask from his jacket pocket. 'Take a good swig of this.'

'Why, thank you,' said the priest, taking a long draught. 'My, my, that's awfully good whiskey.'

'Have another,' said the minister. 'It'll do you the world of good.'

'Thank you, I will,' said the priest. 'But aren't you having any yourself?'

'Certainly not,' said the minister, retrieving the flask. 'Here come the police.'

Ian Paisley walked into his church one Sunday afternoon and found a Catholic on his knees in the aisle.

'What are you doing there, man?' he roared.

'Scrubbing the floor, Mr Paisley,' said the Catholic.

'That's all right,' said Paisley, 'But God help you if I catch you praying.'

Downtown Radio newsflash. . . 'An intruder was seen leaving a store in Belfast early today with his hand in flames. Police are looking for a man with an Armalite.'

A Ballymena man got on the bus in Belfast and nearly had a fit when he was told that the fare was 45p. He had a fierce argument with the driver until finally the driver got so exasperated that he stopped the bus, picked up the Ballymena man's suitcase and flung it out of the door and into the River Lagan.

'Holy God,' said the Ballymena man. 'First you try to rob me, now you try to drown my son.'

A frantic motorist ran into Donegall Pass police station in Belfast.

'Oh officer,' he cried. 'I've just run over a student. What can I do?'

'I'm sorry, sir,' said the policeman. 'It's Sunday, so you can't collect the reward until tomorrow.'

An English atheist came to Strabane for his holidays, met Attracta, fell in love with her and got married. The first Sunday after the wedding Attracta dragged him out of bed and off to their first Mass together.

Naturally, he didn't have a clue about all the rituals involved, and Attracta had to constantly whisper: 'Stand up, sit down, kneel, stand up again, kneel. . .'

Sweating from all the activity, he took out his handkerchief and wiped his brow, then laid it on his lap to dry. Attracta noticed this and she leaned over.

'Is your fly open?' she said.

'No,' he said. 'Should it be?'

Two prisoners in the Maze developed a brilliant system of communicating with each other by tapping messages on the wall in Morse code. But the system fell to pieces when they were moved to separate cells.

Wee Sammy comes running into the kitchen.

'Mammy, Mammy,' he says, 'I want to get married to Jimmy next door.'

'Don't be silly,' says his mother. 'It's impossible.'

'But why, Mammy? I love him.'

'Yer daddy will tell you when he gets home.'

So Sammy's daddy arrives home, and wee Sammy runs up to him.

'Daddy, Daddy, I want to marry wee Jimmy next door.'

'I know,' says his daddy. 'Your mother told me.'

'Well, can I?' asks wee Sammy.

'Certainly not,' says his daddy. 'It would never work.'

'Why not, Daddy?'

'Because he's a Catholic.'

Alliance Party headquarters was blown up last night. Party spokesman Basil Glass said he was shattered.

Old Sammy was lying on his deathbed in Ballymena. Maisie came in and knelt gently beside the bed.

'Sammy,' she asked, 'Do you have any last wishes?'

'Och, Maisie, that's very kind,' said Sammy. 'You know, I was thinking that I wouldn't mind a piece of thon boiled ham on the table.'

'Now, Sammy,' said Maisie, 'you know very well that ham's for the funeral.'

'Right, Jimmy,' said Miss, 'I want you to use a sentence with the word "bakelite" in it, for the class.'

'Please, Miss,' said Jimmy, 'my dad fell asleep last night with his pipe in his mouth and set his bake alight.'

What's the most exciting job in west Belfast?
Rear gunner on a milk float.

A Ballymena man was chatting up a girl at a party.

'Didn't I hear vaguely somewhere that your father died and left you £5,364,278.34½?' he said.

Cedric and Cecil from Bangor were camping in the forest. One day Cedric went to get water and didn't come back.

Three weeks later he staggered into the campsite in an awful state – clothes ripped off, thin as a rake.

'My God,' said Cecil, 'whatever happened?'

'Oh, it was awful,' said Cedric. 'I was on my way to get water when this enormous gorilla leapt out and had his way with me. I was so disorientated that I've been wandering around since then trying to find my way back here.'

'Are you hurt?' asked Cecil.

'Hurt?' sobbed Cedric. 'Of course I'm hurt! It's been three weeks, and he hasn't phoned, he hasn't written. . .'

Kevin was the CO of the IRA training camp hidden deep in the Sperrins, and he was a fearsome disciplinarian. One day he had the men out marching – 'Left right, left right, left right' – when there came this 'Atchoo!' from the ranks.

'Halt!' he roared. 'Who sneezed?'

There was no answer but the soft whisper of the wind in the heather.

'Right, Liam,' he said to his second in command. 'Take out your Armalite and mow down everyone in the front row.'

Ratatatatatatatat went Liam's Armalite, and all the volunteers in the front row dropped down dead.

'Now,' said Kevin, 'who sneezed?'

Still there was only silence.

'Again, Liam,' said Kevin. *Ratatatatatatatatat* went Liam's Armalite, and everyone in the second row fell down dead.

'Now,' said Kevin, 'who sneezed?'

Patrick, a timid little crature, stepped out from the end of the last row.

'Sir,' he said, 'it was me who sneezed.'

'Bless you, Patrick,' said Kevin, 'Left right, left right, left right.'

Did you hear about the Ulster Euro-MP? He was illiterate in two languages.

What's the Ulster definition of foreplay?
'Brace yourself, Bridget.'

A Ballymena man was walking down the street when another one rushed up to him.

'Are you the man who dived into the river to save my wee son?' said the man.

'Aye, I am.'

'Well, where's his cap?'

What's Gerry Adams' bodyguard called?

Liam O'Loan.

Six Strabane men piled out of a pub, barely able to walk, and started to climb into a Mini.

'You drive, Liam,' said Kevin, 'You're too drunk to sing.'

'Sammy,' said Billy, 'did you hear what happened to Jimmy?'

'What?'

'He dropped dead outside a Linfield match.'

'Coming out or going in?'

'Going in.'

'God, that's awful.'

A Belfast man, a Derry man and a Ballymena man go for a splash-up meal at the Culloden Hotel. As they're getting up from the table, the Ballymena man says: 'It's all right, everyone, I'll get the bill.'

The headline on the front page of the next day's *Irish News* read: 'Belfast ventriloquist kicked to death in hotel foyer'.

A Derry man went to see a psychiatrist.

'Doctor,' he said. 'is it possible to become infatuated with an elephant?'

'Of course not,' said the doctor. 'Don't be silly.'

'Well, in that case,' said the Derry man, 'do you know anyone who's looking for an extra large engagement ring?'

'Son, will you look after your oul' mammy when I'm old and grey?'

'Why, Mammy, what'll you be doing?'

A Ballymena shopkeeper lay dying in bed with his family gathered around him.

'Are you there, Sadie?' he called plaintively.

'I'm here, Sammy,' said his wife, taking his hand.

'Are you there, Ian?'

'I'm here, daddy.'

'Are you there, Maisie?'

'I'm here, daddy.'

'Is everyone here, Sadie?'

'Yes, darling, everyone's here.'

'Well, then, who the hell's minding the shop?'

This fella spent an hour wandering aimlessly around a gent's outfitter's in Newtownards before approaching the shopkeeper.

'Listen,' he said, 'have you none of those dunchers with the peak at the back?'

It was a bitterly cold winter in Ballymena, and the teacher was warning the children to be careful about wrapping up well.

'My neighbour's little boy went out on his sledge in the snow and caught pneumonia, and within three days he was dead,' she said.

'Where's his sledge, miss?' came a voice from the back of the class.

Two Strabane men were working on a building site laying pipes. When they'd finished filling in, they still had a large pile of earth left over.

'I wonder how that happened?' said Liam.

'We mustn't have dug the hole deep enough,' said Kevin.

Liam was sitting in his favourite seat in a pub in Derry when Pat walked in beaming all over his face.

'Hello, Pat,' said Liam. 'What has you looking so happy?'

'It's me deafness,' said Pat. 'I've been deaf for as long as I can remember, and now they've invented this new hearing aid which has cured me completely.'

'That's amazing,' said Liam. 'And how much did it cost?'

'Half past three.'

Did you hear about the Derry man who made a million? He bought a row of corner shops.

This Belfast woman had been standing at the bar in a pub on the Ormeau Road for an hour, tapping her fingers impatiently. Finally the door opened and her husband walked in, looking hot and bothered.

'I'm sorry I'm so late, love,' he said. 'There's bomb scares everywhere and the whole place is accordioned off.'

Two ninety-year-olds stagger into a Belfast solicitor's office and ask for a divorce.

'A divorce?' says the solicitor. 'How long have you been married?'

'Seventy years,' says the old man.

'And why are you getting a divorce after all this time?'

'Can't stand the sight of each other,' says the woman. 'Never could.'

'Well,' asks the solicitor, 'why didn't you get divorced years ago, then?'

'It was for the sake of the children,' says the old man. 'We wanted to wait until they were dead.'

An Ulsterman, a Scotsman and a German were all mercenaries in South America, fighting for Freedonia against neighbouring Nirvana, when they were captured one night in the mountains by the Nirvanians.

Now, the Nirvanians were a nasty lot, and their favourite method of passing the time while waiting for the next shipment of arms from President Reagan was to absentmindedly whip a few prisoners to death with a couple of lengths of barbed wire.

Not surprisingly, Seamus, McTavish and Klaus spent a sleepless night and at dawn they were hauled into a clearing in the middle of the tents, where lengths of barbed wire lay glinting cruelly in the light of the rising sun.

The Nirvanian leader stamped up to McTavish. 'You first, Scotsman,' he said. 'And since I'm in a good mood this morning, on account of it being my birthday, you can have a last request before we whip you.'

'Thank you very much,' said the Scotsman. 'If you go to my haversack, you will find there a bottle of the finest single malt. Perhaps you would be kind enough to pour it over my back before you start in with the barbed wire.'

So the Scotch was got and poured over the Scotsman's back, and two of the Nirvanian minions set to with the lengths of razor-sharp steel. But by noon there was hardly a dent in McTavish's back, and the two minions dropped dead with exhaustion. The rebel leader, convinced that it was an omen from the Gods, pardoned him, and McTavish was led away to a tent, moaning slightly at the thought of a whole bottle of Scotch down the drain.

'Well, my German friend,' said the rebel leader, 'now it's your turn. And while I'm not in quite such a good mood as I was this morning, I suppose you'd better have your last request as well.'

'*Danke schön*,' said Klaus, clicking his immaculately polished heels together. 'If you go to my haversack, there you will find a bottle of the finest Bavarian *apfelschnapps*. Perhaps you would be kind enough to douse my back with it before the whipping starts.'

So the schnapps was brought and poured, and the whipping started. Well, this time there were three teams of them, whipping in relays. They whipped all that day and all that night and all the next morning, and by noon the next day there wasn't even a hint of a suspicion of a scratch on the German's back. Furious, the rebel leader had him led away, and turned to Seamus.

'Well, my fine Ulsterman,' he said, 'and what would you like on your back while we whip you for the next week?'

'The German, please,' said Seamus.

Ian Paisley was walking down Church Street in Ballymena when a well-dressed man got out of a Mercedes, rushed up to him and shook his hand.

'Mr Paisley, sir,' he said, 'I want to thank you from the bottom of my heart.'

'Oh?' said Paisley. 'Why's that?'

'It's like this,' said the man. 'Three years ago I was on the verge of bankruptcy when I went to one of your sermons about temperance. It was the one about the alcoholic who spent all his money in the tavern, so that his wife and children went about barefoot, while the family of the tavern owner dressed in the finest silks and linens.'

'Ah, yes, I remember that one well,' said Paisley. 'And you're telling me that you gave up the drink there and then and turned to the narrow path of righteousness, is that it?'

'Not at all,' said the man. 'I'm telling you that I got a bank loan and bought a pub.'

A man phones up Cliftonville Football ground and asks for twenty tickets for Saturday's game.

'Twenty?' says the club secretary. 'Are you sure you didn't want Linfield or somewhere?'

'Oh no,' says the man. 'Cliftonville it is. Can I get the twenty tickets all right?'

'Of course you can.'

'And what time does the game start?'

'What time can you and your friends get here?'

A drunken stranger walked into a lonely pub in the Sperrins and shouted at the top of his voice: 'Maggie Thatcher's face looks like the back end of a sheep.'

The locals descended on him in a rage, and he was left lying outside in an awful state.

'I wouldn't have thought this was Tory country,' he moaned to a passer-by.

'It's not,' said the passer-by. 'It's sheep country.'

A drunk walked into a bar in Ballymena.

'Was I in here last night?' he asked the barman.

'You were indeed, Sandy,' he said.

'Did I spend much money?'

'Oh, about £40.'

'Thank goodness for that. I thought I'd lost it.'

'I've got a joke on you,' said the Derry man. 'You didn't pull the curtains last night and I saw you in bed with your wife.'

'The joke's on you,' said the other Derry man. 'I wasn't in last night.'

Two Bangor women were sitting chatting in the hairdresser's.

'Do you think women prefer conceited men or the other kind?' asked Samantha.

'What other kind?' asked Jane.

Where's the best place to buy a house in Belfast?
British Home Stores.

A wee Belfast boy came home from school in tears.

'What's the matter, son?' asked his mammy.

'We were doing sums today, Mammy,' he said.

'And were they too hard?'

'Well, the teacher said either I couldn't count, or I was stupid, or all three.'

Four Stranocum men were killed drinking milk yesterday.

The cow fell over.

A survey by the Northern Ireland Office has just revealed what Ballymena men do with old razor blades.

Shave.

Seamus walked into the pub in Belfast and sat down at the bar beside Tom, who was looking particularly gloomy.

'What's the matter, Tom?' he asked.

'I've just been to the doctor,' said Tom. 'I've only got a few months to live.'

'What is it?' said Seamus.

Tom leaned over so that no one could hear, and spelt out: 'A-I-D-S.'

'You think you've got problems?' said Seamus. 'I've only got twenty-four hours to live.'

'What is it?' asked Tom.

Seamus leaned over and whispered in his ear: 'I-N-L-A.'

'Da,' asked the Belfast five-year-old, 'what makes children delinquent?'

'Shut up, son. Pour yourself another drink and deal.'

The Black and Tans lifted O'Reilly and dragged him off to the gallows in the pouring rain.

'That's an awful day, isn't it?' he remarked to the hangman.

'You're lucky,' said the hangman. 'I've got to walk home in it.'

It was the eve of the Battle of Hastings, and King Harold was inspecting the archers.

'Right,' he said to Clive from Surrey. 'Show me what you can do with your longbow.'

'You see that almighty oak a hundred yards away?' said Clive from Surrey. 'You see that rook perched in its topmost branch? Watch this.'

He took a fine shaft from his quiver, took aim in a second, and loosed it. *Ssssssssssfth*. A hundred yards away, the rook fell down dead with the arrow through its heart.

'Excellent,' said Harold. 'Tomorrow you shall be in the front rank of the archers.' And he passed on to McTavish, one of his finest Scottish volunteers.

'Well, McTavish,' said Harold. 'Are we as good north of the border?'

'You see that stile five hundred yards away?' said McTavish. 'You see that field mouse perched upon it? Watch this.'

In the twinkling of an eye a shaft was winging through the air, and three fields away the field mouse fell with an arrow through its heart.

'Excellent,' said Harold. 'You shall be in the front row tomorrow, shoulder to shoulder with Clive.' And he passed on to Jimmy from Belfast, the only Ulsterman in his entire army.

'Well, Jimmy,' said Harold, 'Are we as good across the water?'

Jimmy got to his feet.

'You see that barn door five yards away?' he said.

'I do,' said Harold.

'Watch this,' said Jimmy, struggling to get his arrow out of the quiver. A minute later, he took aim and loosed his shaft. It missed the barn door by half a mile and landed several hedges away.

'For God's sake, Jimmy,' said Harold, 'stay at the back tomorrow or you'll put somebody's eye out.'

The phone rings at Purdysburn.

'Hello, who's in Room 34?'

'There's no one in Room 34.'

'Hooray, I've escaped!'